Born in Brooklyn, New [illegible] man was trained as a percussionist f[illegible] taught in New York for fifteen years, du[illegible] time he also taught drums privately, and wrote c[illegible]ren's books and music tuition books for percussion instruments. His music books are among the bestselling drum tuition books in the USA and sell worldwide. He now lives in London and has turned his full attention to writing humour books for both children and adults.

Help! I've Changed My Mind!

Joel Rothman

Illustrations by
Peter Dredge

Fontana/Collins

First published in 1985 by Fontana Paperbacks,
8 Grafton Street, London W1X 3LA

Made and printed in Great Britain by
William Collins Sons & Co. Ltd, Glasgow

My husband took his own life.
That was very thoughtful of him!
GREGG

I feel like drowning myself but I couldn't stand the thought of seeing my life flash before my eyes!

I'd kill myself if I wasn't so sure it would make my wife deliriously happy.
ORESSE

Must go now, Mother, George has just taken poison in a temporary fit of sanity!

That's right – Fred and I had a bet as to which one of us would die first and the bum killed himself just so I would lose the bet!
ORLOSE

This is another instance of a civil servant taking his own life. He left a note in triplicate.
ORCOOZ

If you're going to jump do it at the other end of the bridge. A splash here will scare the fish away!
ORTOOLE

Sorry — I can't go today. My half brother's just taken his own life.
Well then — how about playing just nine holes?
ORLOGE

You twit — can't you do anything right!
DREDGE

Suicide – the sincerest form of self-criticism.

Poison – what you take when you can't take it any longer.

Dear, sir —— in determining whether it was suicide or an accident, I must remind you that the deceased was playing Russian roulette with all the chambers loaded!
CORONER
GREGG

Just what do you think you're doing? The grass hasn't been mowed!

You keep saying you've given me the best years of your life — in that case why not end it now?

What's the water like?

Remember the nanny that took care of you when you were a baby? Well she killed herself!
I guess you might say the hand that rocked the cradle kicked the bucket!

I'm a health freak — this is the way I want to go. I'm going to jog myself to death. I'll be happier and healthier!

I was thinking of killing myself but my husband has given me the will to live — he wants a divorce!

LOVERS
LEAP
DREDGE

I'm here to see the grave of my husband, Harry Cohen.
I'm afraid we don't have a Harry Cohen — only a Jessie Cohen!
That's him — before he shot himself he put everything in my name!

'Dont jump!' yelled the Irish priest to a man on the ledge of a building. 'Think of your wife and children.'

'I've got no wife or children,' shouted the man.

'Then think of your parents.'

'My parents are dead.'

'Then think of your friends at work.'

'I have no job.'

'Then think of St Patrick.'

'Who's St Patrick?'

'Jump, you bastard!'

That reminds me — we're having a barbecue this weekend. Can you come?
PETROL

Your husband's last request before killing himself was that I'd flick his ashes all over the new carpet!

Trust you to take the easy way out, dear!

I'll be with you in a minute, darling — just doing my face!
LOVERS LEAP

Great news — you know those Joneses you're always trying to keep up with — well she's just taken her own life!

Doesn't look very quick to me, dear!
DANGER
QUICK SAND!
DREDGE

How many times have I told Trevor that jump-suits aren't really him!
BONA FASHIONS LTD
ORLOBE

On second thoughts...
LOVERS LEAP

If the Prime Minister was to commit suicide, who officiates?
The undertaker!
ORECBE

A man took his own life, and after a brief investigation his wife had him cremated. She kept his ashes in an urn on the coffee table in front of the couch. When friends came to visit her they would sometimes flick their cigarette and cigar ashes into the urn, forgetting that it contained the remains of her dead husband. One day, as the widow was dusting the urn, she looked inside and thought to herself, 'Is it just my imagination, or is Fred putting on weight?'

If you don't marry me I'll kill myself!
That's very considerate of you!
O'RECOBE

We don't hear from too many people — perhaps we should install a phone?
SAMARITANS
DRESSE

Having committed suicide, Mr Hawkins leaves a will which states: 'Being of sound mind I've spent every last penny I had before dying!'
LAST WILL + TESTAMEN

This time we jump together!
LOVERS LEAP

Our neighbour committed suicide by taking an overdose of laxatives!
Shit! What a way to go!
ORGOBE

It's just been confirmed that a man who was attempting suicide by lying across British Rail tracks eventually died of exposure!
NEWSFLASH

At least use a silencer, George — you don't want to wake the children!
ORCOBE

This is a new one on me, officer — committing suicide by standing in a bath of acid!
ORECOBE

Did your rich boyfriend remember you in his will before he killed himself?
He must have — he left me out!
ORECCHE

A not-so-bright husband arrived home early from work to discover his wife in bed with another man. He became so infuriated that he got out his pistol and pointed the gun at his own head. The wife and her lover began laughing hysterically. 'What are you laughing at?' yelled the husband. 'Both of you are next!'

You and your suicide attempts —— have you seen this month's gas bill?
GAS BILL
DREDGE

INLAND REVENUE
Jump! Jump!
ORDGE

It's tough losing a wife through suicide, son. One day you'll find someone else and remarry.
Maybe — but in the meantime, what am I going to do tonight?
HERE LIES

There now Mrs Clancy – your husband took his own life and it's hard on you. We never realize the full value of anything until we lose it.
Yes, Father – and I certainly won't realize anything. The son of a bitch wasn't insured!
ORLOBE

It was selfish of your husband to take his own life. What am I going to do now for sex?
TREDGE

SWINGING
HANG
'A'
GRAM

I hear Fred took his own life. Did he leave his wife much?
Nearly every night!
DREDGE

Not on my best carpet!
ORLOFF

A man shot himself in the head. When a doctor arrived and saw the man in a pool of blood on the floor he pronouced him dead. 'I'm not dead,' moaned the man on the floor in a very low voice. 'Hush, dear,' replied the wife as she bent over her husband. 'The doctor knows best.'

One minister was eulogizing a man who took his own life. He said, 'We have here only the shell – the nut is gone!'

I'm thinking of committing suicide!
Well you can do it by taking an overdose, hanging, gassing yourself or eating my wife's cooking!

I'm tired of living, James — drive me over a cliff!
ORLOBE

It appears he choked to death on his suicide note!

It's your wife —
will you be home
for supper?

How did you know your dad was really dead after he shot himself?
He didn't move when I kicked him!

Now that your husband has killed himself, would you like him embalmed, cremated or buried?
All three — I'm taking no chances!
EMBALMINGS
CREMATIONS
BURIALS

Just a minute Miss Prigley – you haven't finished work yet!

Darling, do you want a change of underwear before you go?
O'REGGIE

My Harry took a gun and blew his brains out.
Knowing your husband, he must have been a bloody good shot!
BUS STOP

LOVERS LEAP
ORECUE